God's Purpose for Me

Loveland, Colorado

Group's R.E.A.L. Guarantee to you:

This Group resource incorporates our R.E.A.L. approach to ministry—one that encourages long-term retention and life transformation. It's ministry that's:

Relational
  Because learner-to-learner interaction enhances learning and builds Christian friendships.

Experiential
  Because what learners experience through discussion and action sticks with them up to 9 times longer than what they simply hear or read.

Applicable
  Because the aim of Christian education is to equip learners to be both hearers and doers of God's Word.

Learner-based
  Because learners understand and retain more when the learning process takes into consideration how they learn best.

God's Purpose for Me
Faith 4 Life
Junior High Bible Study Series

Copyright © 2003 Group Publishing, Inc.

All rights reserved. No part of this book may be reproduced in any manner whatsoever without prior written permission from the publisher, except where noted in the text and in the case of brief quotations embodied in critical articles and reviews. For information, write Permissions, Group Publishing, Inc., Dept. PD, P.O. Box 481, Loveland, CO 80539.

Visit our Web site: **www.grouppublishing.com**

Credits
Contributing Authors: Rick Chromey, Cindy S. Hansen, and Siv M. Ricketts
Editor: Amy Simpson
Creative Development Editor: Dave Thornton
Chief Creative Officer: Joani Schultz
Copy Editor: Loma Huh
Art Director: Sharon Anderson
Cover Art Director: Jeff A. Storm
Cover Photograqpher: Daniel Treat
Print Production Artist: Tracy K. Donaldson
Illustrators: Matt Wood and Alan Flinn
Production Manager: DeAnne Lear

Unless otherwise noted, Scripture taken from the HOLY BIBLE, NEW INTERNATIONAL VERSION®. Copyright © 1973, 1978, 1984 by International Bible Society. Used by permission of Zondervan Publishing House. All rights reserved.

ISBN 0-7644-2497-1
10 9 8 7 6 5 4 3 2   12 11 10 09 08 07 06 05 04 03

Printed in the United States of America.

Table of Contents

5 · Introduction

9 · Study 1: Knowing God's Will
The Point: God has given us several ways to know his will.
Scripture Source: Jeremiah 29:11-13   Matthew 5:1-12

17 · Study 2: Doing God's Will
The Point: You can do God's will with your heart, soul, body, and mind.
Scripture Source: Matthew 22:37-40   Galatians 5:13-15

25 · Study 3: A Code to Live By
The Point: God wants you to have integrity.
Scripture Source: Daniel 6

35 · Study 4: What Really Matters
The Point: Our commitment to God is what really matters.
Scripture Source: Matthew 13:1-9, 18-23

45 · Changed 4 Life

God's Purpose for Me

Knowing God's purpose for them helps young people make good decisions about their future, moral issues, and even day-to-day concerns.

Today's junior highers want to know the answers to a lot of different questions: questions about the future, questions of right or wrong, and questions about day-to-day issues. They'll probably face tough decisions in each of these areas as they grow into adulthood. They need guidance, but often they don't know where to find that guidance.

Knowing God's purpose for them helps young people make good decisions about their future, moral issues, and even day-to-day concerns. Knowing God's purpose can transform the way they see themselves, others, and the importance of their choices.

In this book, teenagers will come to an understanding of how to live according to God's purpose for them, both for the present and for the future. In the first study, they'll learn about some concrete methods for discovering God's will.

In the second study, students will learn how to follow God's will in various areas of their lives. In doing so, they'll learn how to obey God's greatest commandments.

In the third study, teenagers will have the opportunity to discover that purpose has less to do with *what* we do than with *how* we do it. Students will be encouraged to live with integrity.

Finally, they'll take a look at their ultimate purpose in life—growing in relationship with God. They'll consider how the busyness and distractions of life can keep them from fulfilling that purpose.

Giving your students an understanding of God's purpose for them can provide an internal compass which helps give them direction in every area of life. As they carry this understanding with them, they'll be transformed inside and out.

junior high bible study series

About Faith 4 Life

Use Faith 4 Life studies to show your teenagers how the Bible is relevant to their lives. Help them see that God can invade every area of their lives and change them in ways they can only imagine. Encourage your students to go deeper into faith—faith that will sustain them for life! Faith 4 Life, forever!

Faith 4 Life: Junior High Bible Study Series helps young teenagers take a Bible-based approach to faith and life issues. Each book in the series contains these important elements:

■ **Life application of Bible truth**—Faith 4 Life studies help teenagers understand what the Bible says and then apply that truth to their lives.

■ **A relevant topic**—Each Faith 4 Life book focuses on one main topic, with four studies to give your students a thorough understanding of how the Bible relates to that topic. These topics were chosen by youth leaders as the ones most relevant for junior high–age students.

■ **One point**—Each study makes one point, centering around that one theme to make sure students really understand the important truth it conveys. This point is stated upfront and throughout the study.

■ **Simplicity**—The studies are easy to use. Each contains a "Before the Study" box that outlines any advance preparation required. Each study also contains a "Study at a Glance" chart so you can quickly and easily see what supplies you'll need and what each study will involve.

■ **Action and interaction**—Each study relies on experiential learning to help students learn what God's Word has to say. Teenagers discuss and debrief their experiences in large groups, small groups, and individual reflection.

■ **Reproducible handouts**—Faith 4 Life books include reproducible handouts for students. No need for student books!

■ **Tips, tips, and more tips**—Faith 4 Life studies are full of "FYI" tips for the teacher, providing extra ideas, insights into young people, and hints for making the studies go smoothly.

■ **Flexibility**—Faith 4 Life studies include optional activities and bonus activities. Use a study as it's written, or use these options to create the study that works best for your group.

■ **Follow-up ideas**—At the end of each book, you'll find a section called "Changed 4 Life." This section provides ideas for following up with your students to make sure the Bible truths stick with them.

Knowing God's Will

Many teenagers desire to follow God but don't know how. They hear conflicting advice from many different sources. People say, "Just follow God's will," but junior highers don't really know what that means. And they sometimes have trouble knowing what God would have them do.

God didn't leave us alone to just guess at what he wants for us. He wants us to understand his desires for us. This study can help junior highers see a glimpse of God's will for their lives. Assure them that God has not deserted them! He'll let them know what he wants them to do if they seek him sincerely.

The Point

▶ God has given us several ways to know his will.

Scripture Source

Jeremiah 29:11-13
God tells the captives in Babylon that he has a plan for them.

Matthew 5:1-12
Jesus gives us guidelines for living.

The Study at a Glance

Warm-Up (10-15 minutes)

Blind Search
What students will do: Play a game that illustrates "blindly searching" for God's will.
Needs: ❑ blindfold

Optional Activity (10-15 minutes)

What students will do: See how a blindfolded person struggles to find a Bible.
Needs: ❑ Bible
❑ blindfold

Bible Connection (20-25 minutes)

Ways to God's Will
What students will do: Complete a handout and learn ways to seek God's will.
Needs: ❑ "This Way to God's Will!" handouts (p. 14)
❑ pens

Life Application (15-20 minutes)

Fitting It All Together
What students will do: Write and pray over what they'll do to seek God's will.
Needs: ❑ "God's Will Puzzle" handouts (p. 15)
❑ scissors
❑ pens
❑ envelopes

Before the Study →

Make one photocopy of the "This Way to God's Will!" handout (p. 14) for each person.

For the "Ways to God's Will" activity, be prepared to share a story of how God has helped you make a decision using prayer, the Bible, others, or the church.

Photocopy and cut apart a puzzle for each student from the "God's Will Puzzle" handout (p. 15). Put each cut-up puzzle in a separate envelope.

Warm-Up

Blind Search
(10 to 15 minutes)

Begin by choosing one junior higher to be the searcher. Blindfold that person and have him or her stand in the middle of the room. Have the other teenagers scatter around the edges of the room, each standing an arm's length away from any other person—if that's possible in your classroom.

Once teenagers are in their places, instruct them to not move their feet and to remain absolutely quiet. Then spin the searcher around three times, and tell him or her to take five steps forward. If the searcher touches someone, that person trades places with the searcher. If not, give the searcher a few more spins in that spot and let him or her try again. Keep going until at least four or five teenagers have had a chance to be the searcher.

ASK:

■ How did it feel to be the searcher?

■ When have you felt that way in real life?

■ How is that kind of searching like searching for God's will in your life?

SAY:

The Point ▶

■ Sometimes it seems like we're groping blindly when we search for God's will. But <u>God has given us several ways to know his will</u>. Today we're going to look at some ways we can find what God wants for our lives.

*⃰ Optional Activity

(10 to 15 minutes)

Instead of the "Blind Search" activity, try this variation.

Begin by sending one teenager out of the room while you give directions to the other teenagers. Place a Bible at some out-of-the-way place in the room. Then form three groups. Tell one group to shout directions that would lead the searcher away from the Bible. Tell another group to shout random directions, some toward the Bible and some away from it. Tell the third group to shout directions toward the Bible. Tell teenagers they can only use the following directional commands: "forward," "backward," "right," "left," "up," and "down."

Then blindfold your searcher, bring him or her back into the room, and signal the teenagers to start shouting their directions.

Afterward,

ASK:
- How did it feel to be the searcher?
- When have you felt that way in real life?
- How is that kind of searching like searching for God's will in your life?

SAY:
- Sometimes it seems really confusing when we search for God's will. But <u>God has given us several ways to know his will</u>. Today we're going to look at some ways we can find what God wants for our lives.

◀ **The Point**

Ways to God's Will
(20 to 25 minutes)

SAY:
- It's not always easy to know exactly what God wants for us. Some things are clearly spelled out for us in the Bible while others aren't. But even with the tough decisions, <u>God has</u>

The Point ▶ <u>given us several ways to help us discern what he would have us choose</u>.

Distribute the "This Way to God's Will!" handouts (p. 14) and pens. Form four groups. A group can be one person. Assign one section of the handout

Bible Connection

At the end of the "Ways to God's Will" activity, be sure you have a life experience of your own ready to share as a starter. You'll probably need to go first to get the sharing time rolling.

to each group, and have groups read their Scriptures and answer the questions related to their topics. Then have groups report their findings to the rest of the class while class members fill in answers on their handouts.

When the groups have reported, ask volunteers to share how God has helped them make a decision using at least one of the ways you've just talked about.

Life Application

Fitting It All Together
(15 to 20 minutes)

SAY:

■ **We've seen ways to discover God's will for us. Now let's decide what we're really going to do.**

Distribute pens and the envelopes with the puzzle pieces you cut apart before the study. Have teenagers write on each puzzle piece how they'll use that element when they're puzzled about God's will for them. For example, for prayer someone might write, "I'll pray and open myself to God's answers and direction." For the church, someone might write, "I'll ask my Sunday school teacher for advice, and I'll soak up all the support I can from other Christians."

When teenagers have finished writing on their puzzle pieces, instruct them each to put the pieces together to form a square. When they've finished,

SAY:

■ **When we use all the methods God has given us to seek his will, things will often fit together like the pieces of a puzzle. Even when it doesn't seem like there's a way, God can work it**

The Point ▶ **out. <u>God has given us several ways to know his will.</u>**

Form an "unpuzzled" circle by having teenagers arrange their assembled puzzles in a circle on the floor. Then have the teenagers gather around the circle of puzzles and link arms. Pray together, asking God to help all of you remember to use prayer, others, the Bible, and the church when searching for God's will in your lives. Encourage teenagers to take their puzzles home with them to remind them of what they said they'd do in seeking God's will.

This Way to God's Will!

Read through the passages for your topic and answer the questions related to them.

Prayer
Jeremiah 29:11-13; 1 Thessalonians 5:16-18; and James 1:4-6
- How does prayer help you know God's will for your life?
- List four decisions you're facing in which prayer might help you make the right choice.

_____
_____
_____

The Bible
Exodus 20:1-17; Matthew 5:1-12; and 2 Timothy 3:16-17
- How does the Bible help you know God's will for your life?
- List four decisions you're facing in which the Bible might help you make the right choice.

_____
_____
_____

Others
Proverbs 6:20-23; 11:11, 14; and 1 Thessalonians 5:11-14
- How do others help you know God's will for your life?
- List four decisions you're facing in which other people might help you make the right choice.

_____
_____
_____

The Church
Acts 13:1-3; 2 Thessalonians 1:1-12; and 1 Peter 4:7-11
- How does the church help you know God's will for your life?
- List four decisions you're facing in which the church might help you make the right choice.

_____
_____
_____

Permission to photocopy this handout from Faith 4 Life: Junior High Bible Study Series, *God's Purpose for Me* granted for local church use.
Copyright © Group Publishing, Inc., P.O. Box 481, Loveland, CO 80539. www.grouppublishing.com

God's Will Puzzle

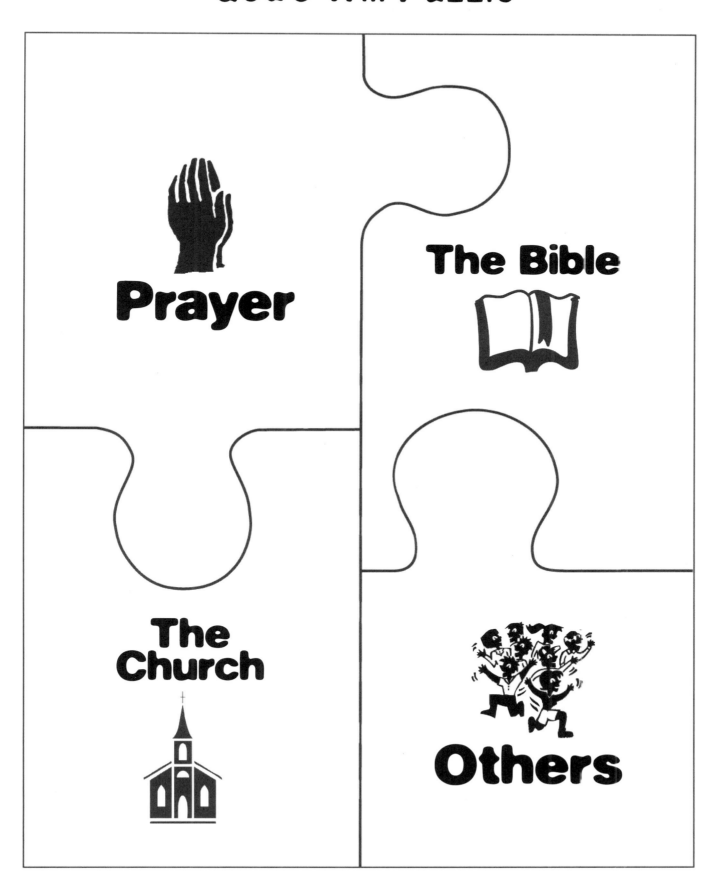

Doing God's Will

Study 2

Part of knowing God's will for the future involves following what we know as his will for our daily lives. And one thing we know about his will is that we're to follow him completely—with our hearts, souls, bodies, and minds. Junior highers need to know that God does want them to follow him in their daily lives. He's not just a God for Sunday or for youth group. He's a God who wants his people to follow him every minute of their lives.

As teenagers learn to follow God in little things daily, they'll be preparing themselves to follow him when bigger decisions come along. Loving the Lord with heart, soul, body, and mind and loving your neighbor as yourself are the "prime directives" of God's will for Christians. And junior highers are ready to begin using their abilities to follow these directives.

17

The Point

▶ You can do God's will with your heart, soul, body, and mind.

Scripture Source

Matthew 22:37-40
Jesus describes the greatest commandment.

Galatians 5:13-15
Paul explains what's most important to God.

The Study at a Glance

Warm-Up (15-20 minutes)

Heart, Soul, Body, and Mind
What students will do: Play a game using the ideas from God's most important commandment.

Bonus Activity (5-10 minutes)

What students will do: Hold a piece of clay or make something from it.
Needs: ❏ modeling clay

Bible Connection (15-20 minutes)

Doing It
What students will do: Think of ways to use their abilities to follow God's will.
Needs: ❏ Bibles
❏ "Doing God's Will" handouts (p. 24)
❏ pens

Life Application (15-20 minutes)

Getting Started
What students will do: Choose a way to follow God this week, and pray that God will help them do what they've committed to do.
Needs: ❏ newsprint
❏ marker
❏ index cards
❏ pens

Before the Study →

Make a photocopy of the "Doing God's Will" handout (p. 24) for each student.

Warm-Up

Heart, Soul, Body, and Mind
(15 to 20 minutes)

When everyone has arrived, start with a discussion.

ASK:

■ When we search for God's will by reading the Bible, listening to others, or praying, what do we hope to discover?

■ Does God's will just relate to our future? Explain.

SAY:

The Point ▶

■ Some parts of God's will are very clear to us from the Bible. And these parts of God's will affect our day-to-day choices. According to the Bible, <u>God wants each of us to love him with our heart, soul, body, and mind</u>. And he wants us to love our neighbors as ourselves. This is God's will for us.

Have teenagers stand in a circle.

SAY:

■ I'm going to read some actions that may be part of doing God's will. If you think an action is related to the heart or emotions, point to your heart. If you think it's related to the soul or spiritual nature, point to the sole of your shoe. If you think it's related to the body or physical nature, flex your arm to make a muscle. If you think it's related to the mind or intellect, point to your brain.

Read the actions from the box on page 20 and let teenagers point. Many of the actions could relate to two or more choices.

STUDY 2 – Doing God's Will

19

Heart, Soul, Body, or Mind?

- forgiving a friend
- going to church
- refusing to take illegal drugs
- deciding to go to college
- helping a brother or sister with homework
- eating healthy foods and exercising
- refusing to repeat gossip
- gathering food to give to the homeless
- trusting in Christ as your Savior

ASK:

- What did you notice about the way people responded to each item?
- How can God's desire for us to love him with our heart, soul, body, and mind affect our choices in the situations we just listed?

SAY:

- We sometimes choose to do negative things with our hearts, souls, bodies, and minds. Let's think about what some of those might be.

Have your teenagers brainstorm some actions for each category: heart, soul, body, and mind—for example, telling someone you hate him or her, denying your faith when talking to a friend, taking drugs, and ignoring school assignments.

SAY:

- When we concentrate on loving God with our heart, soul, body, and mind, and learn to love others as ourselves, we'll more easily be able to avoid those actions that aren't God's will. Now let's think of some of the good actions we might do in following what we know is God's will.

Let teenagers brainstorm good actions for each category: heart, soul, body, and mind—for example, helping a neighbor, praying daily, exercising regularly, and studying for tests.

ASK:

■ How is doing these good actions the same as following God's will?

SAY:

The Point ▶ ■ <u>You can do God's will with your heart, soul, body, and mind.</u> God has given you gifts and abilities to help you do those things that make up his will for you. Let's take a look at some of those gifts and abilities.

✱ Bonus Activity ✱

(5 to 10 minutes)

If you have time, try starting the lesson with this intriguing activity.

As students arrive, give each a lump of modeling clay, but don't give the students any directions. Then go on with your normal opening conversation or simply spend three or four minutes talking about how everyone's doing.

ASK:

■ What did you do with your clay?
■ How is what you did with your clay like the way some people follow God's will?

SAY:

■ You didn't all do the same thing with your clay, and that's OK. That's like the way it is with our lives. God wants each of us to do something different with our lives. Today we're going to look at what it means for each of us to do God's will.

Bible Connection

Doing It
(15 to 20 minutes)

Distribute pens and copies of the "Doing God's Will" handout (p. 24). Have teenagers fill out their handouts.

When they've finished, have students share their ideas for doing God's will.

SAY:

■ <u>You can do God's will with your heart, soul, body, and mind.</u>   ◀ **The Point**

Then have someone read aloud Galatians 5:13-14.

ASK:

■ How does this verse describe doing God's will?
■ What warning does this passage give us about not following God's will?

Getting Started
(15 to 20 minutes)

Life Application

SAY:

■ <u>God wants us to do his will with all of our being—with our</u>   ◀ **The Point**
<u>heart, soul, body, and mind.</u> And there are lots of ways to do
that. Let's brainstorm some we haven't mentioned already.

Have someone from your group list the ideas on newsprint as
they're suggested. Ask teenagers to be specific.

After you have ten or more new ideas listed, distribute index cards
and pens.

SAY:

■ Now choose a way you're going to follow God's will this
week. It can be one of these or one we talked about earlier.
On one side of the card, write a brief description of what
you're going to do. Someone else will be reading your card.

Allow a minute for teenagers to write, then have them form pairs.

SAY:

■ Now turn your card over and write a brief note congratulat-
ing your partner for how you've seen him or her following
God's will in his or her life. For example, you could write,
"Congratulations, Chris! You do God's will in your life by being friendly and making everyone feel welcome." After
you've written the note, give the card to your partner.

> **FYI**
>
> As teenagers are
> sharing ideas for
> doing God's will, be
> sure no ideas are
> criticized. Point out
> that this is a brain-
> storming session
> and it's OK to call
> out any ideas.

After pairs have shared their congratulations, have them talk about what they wrote on the other side of the cards and agree to pray for each other about what they'll do to follow God's will.

SAY:

■ **God never asks us to do something we're incapable of doing. However, we often do need his help in following his will. So let's pray together, asking God to help us do the things we've committed to do. As we pray, ask God to help you specifically with what you chose to do. If you wrote on your card that you'll quit squabbling with your sister, tell God that and ask him to help you with it.**

Allow time for volunteers to pray aloud, then wrap up the class with your own prayer, also telling what you committed to do. Encourage partners to check with each other in the following weeks to see how each other is doing.

Doing God's Will

Read Matthew 22:37-40. Jesus says we should love God with all our heart. What are ways you can use your abilities and gifts to do that? Write your ideas in the heart. For example, you might write, "Look for new students who are struggling and be their friend."

Paul taught that we should honor God with our bodies. What are ways you can use your abilities and gifts to do that? Write your ideas in the picture. For example, you might write, "Avoid drugs so I can have a healthy body."

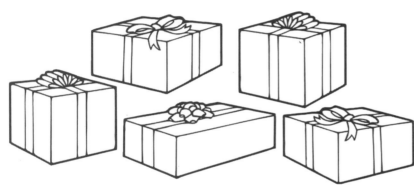

Think about the gifts and abilities God has given you. List at least five in the boxes above. For example, you might write, "good student," "friendly," or "athletic."

Jesus says to love God with all our mind. What are ways you can use your abilities and gifts to do that? Write your ideas in the person's mind. For example, you might write, "Be the best student I can be."

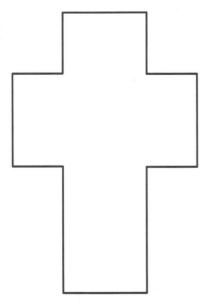

Jesus says to love God with all our soul. What are ways you can use your abilities and gifts to do that? Write your ideas in the cross. For example, you might write, "Invite a friend to a Bible study or youth group."

Jesus says to love your neighbor as yourself. How can you do that using your abilities and gifts? For example, you might write, "Treat all people I meet with respect; listen to them."

_____
_____
_____
_____
_____

A Code to Live By

Study 3

Junior high is a confusing time. As students begin their journey toward adulthood, they're confronted with new responsibilities, exciting privileges, changing bodies, and roller coaster emotions. Amid all this, they're beginning to separate from their parents or guardians and making more of their own decisions about what they will and will not do.

How will they make wise choices?

When confronted with brand-new situations, will your students react with the first response that comes to mind? Or will they have already made all-encompassing decisions about who they'll be and how they'll act in all circumstances?

This study encourages students to define who they want to be and then to create guidelines to live by. As they do this, your young people will discover that God values integrity and explore some ways they can foster integrity in their own lives.

25

The Point

▶ God wants you to have integrity.

Scripture Source

Daniel 6

Daniel demonstrates integrity, remaining faithful to God even when his life is threatened, and God saves him from the lions' den.

The Study at a Glance

Warm-Up (15-20 minutes)

Melting Tag

What students will do: Play Freeze Tag while some students break the rules, then create representations of integrity.

Needs: ❑ dictionaries
❑ assorted art supplies
❑ board game such as Sorry! or Trouble

Bible Connection (20-25 minutes)

No Lion

What students will do: Write "life rules" for characters in Daniel 6, then role-play present-day situations as if they lived by those rules.

Needs: ❑ Bibles
❑ paper
❑ pencils

Life Application (10-15 minutes)

Know the Code

What students will do: Create their own guidelines to live by for the next year.

Needs: ❑ Bibles
❑ paper
❑ pencils
❑ "Live by the Word" handouts (p. 33)

Bonus Activity (up to 5 minutes)

What students will do: Create encouraging decrees about the integrity of their trio members.

Needs: ❑ "Live by the Word" handouts (p. 33)
❑ pencils

Before the Study →

Pull a few students aside, and tell them that the class will play a game of Freeze Tag at the beginning of the study. Instruct these teenagers to not freeze if they're tagged. (In Freeze Tag, people tagged by "It" must stand in place until someone else tags them to set them free.)

Make one photocopy of the "Live by the Word" handout (p. 33) for each person.

Warm-Up

Melting Tag
(15 to 20 minutes)

When everyone has arrived, have one or two people (not the students you talked with before class) volunteer to be "It." Play Freeze Tag for one minute, then

ASK:

- **What was your reaction when you realized some people didn't play by the rules? Why?**
- **Those of you who broke the rules, how did you feel?**
- **How is playing a game and ignoring the rules like believing one thing but doing another? How is it different?**

Have students form trios. As they do, set out dictionaries and a variety of art supplies such as construction paper, assorted colors of markers, glue, magazines, stickers, and tape. The more supplies you provide, the more creative your students can be.

SAY:

- **In your trios, come up with a definition for the word *integrity*. Use the dictionaries I've provided to help you. Once your trio agrees on a definition, create a way to share your definition with the other groups. For example, you could draw a picture about it, tell a story of someone who acted with integrity, or find an object that works because of integrity.**

Give trios three minutes to work. Circulate around the room to help any trios that need it. Then have trios share their representations of integrity with the class.

FYI Make sure you choose enough students to break the rules so others will notice them. For example, if you have fifteen students, you might have three to five teenagers breaking the rules.

When groups have finished sharing, set out a board game and

SAY:

- My representation of integrity is a board game. Having integrity is when you know the rules of the game and live by them.

Have trios discuss these questions:

- When you play a game, do you usually learn the rules at the beginning or figure them out as you play? Why?
- Which is a better way to play? Explain.
- What are some things you believe in? Can your family and friends tell what you believe by the way you act? Why or why not?
- Think of a time you believed in something but acted like you didn't? What happened?

SAY:

- Acting with integrity is difficult when you're not sure what you believe. But if you figure out what you believe before getting into uncertain situations, you can act in line with your beliefs. It's like knowing the rules of the game before you begin playing. <u>God wants you to have integrity</u>, and to- ◀ **The Point** day you'll explore what that means.

 If you have a lot of class time, consider playing the board game during the course of the study. A simple board game such as Sorry! or Trouble will work best.

Start the game by awarding the first turn to the trio with the most creative representation of integrity. Play the game throughout the study by having all groups take a turn after each activity or series of questions.

To create an object lesson for the end of the study, don't explain the game rules until play is well under way. At the end of the study, ask whether it was better to play the game with or without knowing the rules. Then ask whether it might be better to live with or without creating a code to live by.

Bible Connection

No Lion
(20 to 25 minutes)

SAY:

- The story of Daniel gives us an example of a man who lived out exactly what he believed. Daniel was taken from his home and his country when he was about your age and made to work for a foreign king. Although he lived in a strange land with different customs, he remained faithful to the God he had always known, even when his life was in danger.

Designate one corner of the room "Daniel," another corner "Darius," and a third corner "Supervisors." Have trios send one person to each of these corners.

Give each corner group a sheet of paper and a pencil.

SAY:

- Read Daniel 6. Then write the code, the "rules of the game," that your assigned characters lived by. As you work, keep in mind how your characters acted. For example, the Supervisors might have felt embarrassed because Daniel always outshone them. So they might have lived by a rule: "Get rid of anybody who makes us look bad." Create a code that has at least three rules for your characters.

When young people have finished,

SAY:

- Now you're going to become your characters. I'm going to list a series of present-day situations. After I read each situation, act it out with others according to the rules you wrote for your characters.

Call out three or four of the following situations, allowing students to interact with each other for thirty seconds between situations:

- being at a party where there's alcohol
- taking a test at school
- hanging out with friends
- doing chores around the house
- spending an evening with your family
- baby-sitting some neighbor kids

FYI! In Colossians 1:10, Paul tells the Colossians he prays that they will "live a life worthy of the Lord and may please him in every way" and bear "fruit in every good work, growing in the knowledge of God." We all need people who will pray for us and keep us accountable to the goals we set for ourselves. As your young people seek to live lives of integrity, encourage them to find friends who will pray for them and keep them accountable.

STUDY 3 - A Code to Live By

- being approached by a gang at school
- seeing someone you know shoplifting
- playing your rival school in a sport

After the role-plays, have teenagers return to their original trios to discuss these questions:

- **Which of the characters in Daniel's story had the most integrity? Explain.**
- **How did God respond to the integrity level of Daniel? King Darius? the supervisors?**
- **What was it like to act according to a code you'd already written?**
- **How was that like living a life of integrity? How was it different?**
- **Do you have a code you live by? Why or why not?**
- **How could having a code help you have integrity?**
- **How do you think God would respond if you created a code and lived by it?**

SAY:

- **Daniel had integrity, acting according to what he believed. <u>God wants you to have integrity</u> too. Now let's make our own codes to live by.**

◄ **The Point**

> **If you have enough adult leaders, as-sign one to help each group create its codes.**
>
> **FYI**

> **If you have more than fifteen stu-dents, have them form six groups. Assign two groups to each character.**
>
> **FYI**

Know the Code
(10 to 15 minutes)

Life Application

Pass out a "Live by the Word" handout (p. 33), a pencil, and a sheet of paper to each student. Have each person find a place in the room away from others.

SAY:

- **Think about the kind of person you'd like to be. Ask yourself: "If someone were to write a story about how I will live for the next year, what qualities would I want that person to write about?" If you wish, make some notes. Ask God what qualities he'd like you to pursue. You might also want to look up some of the passages on the handout. You won't be able to read them all, but a few of the summaries might spark your interest in reading those passages. As you write,**

30

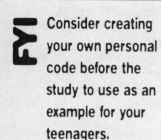

FYI Consider creating your own personal code before the study to use as an example for your teenagers.

be honest—no one will see this but you and God.

After a few minutes,

SAY:

■ Now based on your thoughts and prayer, write a personal code to live by for this year. You can use the Scripture passages on the handout or write something of your own. You can have as many or as few guidelines as you want, but keep them simple so you can remember them easily. They should reflect the kind of person you'd like to be and the steps you'll take to become that person. For example, if you'd like to be a friendly person, you might create guidelines for smiling at people in your school halls and saying "hi" to one new person each week.

After a few minutes, have teenagers stop. If they haven't finished creating their guidelines, encourage teenagers to complete them sometime during the coming week. Then have students return to their trios to pray together that God will help them live lives of integrity in the coming year.

FYI Today's young people value authenticity. You can say whatever you want, but if you don't back up your words with your actions, you'll quickly lose their respect and their attention.

Just as they judge you and other adults, they judge one another. That's why a study about integrity is so important for your teenagers. When your Christian junior highers live out their faith, their friends will respect and listen to them. Their friends may not immediately commit their own lives to Christ, but they'll experience people who remain faithful to God in the midst of a broken world.

Use Daniel's story to help your Christian young people understand that when their actions back up their beliefs, their lives become captivating messages about Jesus. Daniel lived a life of integrity. He didn't change his commitment to God just because the circumstances around him changed. Instead, he faithfully continued his habit of daily prayer, knowing it could cost him his life (Daniel 6:10).

As a result, God was glorified. Daniel still faced the earthly consequences of his obedience to God—King Darius ordered Daniel into the lions' den (verse 16). But God saved Daniel, shutting the lions' mouths (verse 22). God's power to save Daniel from such bleak circumstances powerfully impacted King Darius. He decreed that everyone in his entire kingdom should fear and respect the God Daniel served.

Daniel's faithfulness changed King Darius' life. And your students' integrity can change their friends' lives, too.

* Bonus Activity *

(up to 5 minutes)

If you have time, try closing with this affirmation activity.

When junior highers have finished praying,

SAY:

- **Daniel had integrity when he continued to worship God, even though worshipping someone other than the king put his life in jeopardy. As a result, God spared his life, and King Darius issued a decree that everyone had to fear and respect God.**

- **God wants you to have integrity, just as Daniel did. And just like ◄ The Point Daniel, when your actions match your beliefs, other people notice and are impacted.**

Have each trio sit in a circle. On the back of their "Live by the Word" hand-outs, have each student write a "decree" about how the person to the right has integrity and how that person's integrity has affected his or her life. Then have them read their decrees within their trios and give their decrees to the people they wrote about.

Live by the WORD

Explore some of the passages below as you create your personal code for the year ahead.

exodus 20:1-17
God gives Moses the Ten Commandments, God's **"rules of the game"** for his people.

matthew 5:3-11
Jesus tells us **personality traits and actions** that will make us truly happy.

mark 12:29-31
Jesus commands us to **love God** and our neighbors.

romans 12:9
Paul says that our **love should be real**. We should hate evil and hold onto what's good.

galatians 5:19-23
Paul describes the results of a sinful life and the results of a **relationship with God's Spirit**.

colossians 3:1-10
Paul encourages us to **focus on God** and avoid evil.

james 1:19-22
James gives advice on how to live the **kind of life** God wants us to.

james 4:7-8
James encourages us to **give ourselves completely** to God.

1 peter 1:13-16
Peter says to **be holy** because God is holy.

2 peter 1:3-8
Peter describes **qualities** we should add to our lives because God has greatly blessed us.

Permission to photocopy this handout from Faith 4 Life: Junior High Bible Study Series, *God's Purpose for Me* granted for local church use. Copyright © Group Publishing, Inc., P.O. Box 481, Loveland, CO 80539. www.grouppublishing.com

What Really Matters

4 Study

The teenagers in today's generation are starving spiritually. They sense a deeper meaning to life, and they want to find it.

But they just don't have the time.

Brought up in a fast-paced society where instant gratification is taken for granted, these teenagers ride a bullet train through life. With school, family, friends, and sports, teenagers' daily planners are full, scheduled to the last minute.

When do today's young people "pencil in" time with God? How can they see that God's ultimate purpose for them is to be in a relationship with him? And how can they understand that spiritual growth takes time—a lifetime committed to God?

This study will help your teenagers recognize their need to slow down and invest their time in a lasting pursuit: growing intimate with God.

The Point

▶ Our commitment to God is what really matters.

Scripture Source

Matthew 13:1-9, 18-23

Jesus explains the parable of the sower.

The Study at a Glance

Warm-Up (5-10 minutes)

Buildin' on the Word

What students will do: Stack cups on their Bibles, walk, and read Matthew 6:19-34 at the same time.

Needs:
- ❏ Bibles
- ❏ paper
- ❏ pens
- ❏ paper cups (5 per student)
- ❏ magazines
- ❏ scissors
- ❏ tape
- ❏ table

Optional Activity (5-10 minutes)

What students will do: Juggle various items with group members while reciting Matthew 13:9.

Needs: ❏ various "tossable" items

Bible Connection (25-30 minutes)

Seeds of Change

What students will do: Creatively explore the parable of the seed and the soils and apply what they learn to their lives.

Needs:
- ❏ Bibles
- ❏ "The Seed and the Four Soils" handouts (p. 44)
- ❏ pens

Life Application (15- 20 minutes)

Thirsty Hearts

What students will do: Cut dried sponges into heart shapes, then dip the sponges into water to make them expand.

Needs:
- ❏ Bibles
- ❏ dried sponges
- ❏ airtight plastic bag
- ❏ scissors
- ❏ markers
- ❏ paper cups
- ❏ water

Before the Study →

If you plan to do the "Buildin' on the Word" Warm-Up activity (rather than the Optional Activity), set an eight-foot-long table along one wall of your meeting room. If you'll have more than ten students at your meeting, set two tables along the same wall or form an L-shape in a corner. Set out paper, pens, old magazines, paper cups, scissors, and tape.

If you plan to do the Optional Activity instead, gather several items for teenagers to juggle, such as Ping-Pong balls, baseballs, plastic bottles, stuffed animals, empty soft drink cans, marbles, and small books. Include a variety of shapes and sizes, making sure the items you gather are "tossable" (nothing fragile!). Gather one item per student.

Make a photocopy of the "Seed and the Four Soils" handout (p. 44) for each student.

Gather one (about 4x6-inch) cellulose sponge (available at grocery stores) for every four students in your class. Cut the sponges into four pieces, each measuring about 2x3 inches. Preheat an oven to 200 degrees or less. Place the sponges on the oven rack and let them "bake" for eight to ten minutes. When sponges are thoroughly dried, smash them as flat as possible. If you live in a humid area, you may need to wait and do this just prior to teaching the lesson. Store the dried sponges in an airtight plastic bag.

For every four students, label a paper cup with the phrase "Commitment to God."

Warm-Up

Buildin' on the Word
(5 to 10 minutes)

When everyone has arrived,

SAY:

- Today we're going to discuss how we can focus on God's ultimate purpose for us: to have a relationship with him. To start, take a piece of paper and a pen, then write down the top five situations, people, or things that consume your personal time. For example, family, school, video games, movies, television, pets, or friends might take most of your time.

■ Then search the magazines I've provided for pictures that represent each of your "time consumers." For example, you might find pictures of skateboards, books, or groups of friends. If you can't find just the right pictures, you might find words or letters to spell out your time consumers. Cut out the pictures, words, and letters that best represent each of your time consumers, then tape them to paper cups, one time consumer per cup.

After five minutes, have teenagers stack their cups inside each other and place the stacks on the table you set up earlier. Then have teenagers gather on the opposite side of the room and open their Bibles to Matthew 6:19-34.

SAY:

■ We're going to play a game with our cups. When I say "Go!" read aloud Matthew 6:19-34. As you read, walk to the table, take one cup from your stack, and place the cup somewhere on your open Bible. Then, still reading aloud, return to this end of the room and touch the wall. After you've touched the wall, walk back to the table, take another cup from your stack, and place it on your Bible. You may put one cup on top of the other if you choose, but you may not stack your cups inside each other. Keep reading the Bible passage aloud as you walk to and from the table, placing your cups on your Bible until you've retrieved all five of them. If you have a "cup crash," that's OK. Just put the cups you've already re-trieved back on your Bible and continue with the game. If you come to the end of the Bible passage before you have all five cups, read the passage over again.

Make sure everyone understands the game, then

SAY:

■ Ready? Go!

Allow teenagers to play until each has successfully stacked all five cups on his or her Bible or when the group is having more cup crashes than progress. Then have teenagers form foursomes to discuss these questions:

- What's your reaction to this game?
- How was trying to balance your cups like trying to balance all the activities in your life? How was it different?
- How were the cup crashes like the distractions that keep us from focusing on a relationship with God?
- How was this game like the way your time consumers affect your ultimate purpose in life? How was it different?

Allow five minutes for discussion, then

SAY:

- Today we'll discuss how our activities distract us from God's ultimate purpose for us—growing close to God. Despite all

The Point ▶ the distractions in our lives, <u>our commitment to God is what really matters.</u>

* Optional Activity

(5 to 10 minutes)

Here's another lively game idea you can try with your students instead of the "Buildin' on the Word" activity.

When everyone has arrived, have teenagers form foursomes. Give each student an item to juggle.

SAY:

- Today we're going to discuss how we can focus on God's ultimate purpose for us: to have a relationship with him. To get us thinking about this topic, let's do a little juggling! But before we begin, let's all memorize Matthew 13:9: "He who has ears, let him hear."

Have teenagers turn to a partner within their foursome to help each other memorize the verse. Once everyone can repeat the verse,

SAY:

- Let's begin our juggling game. Find the person in your group with the longest first name (if there are ties, go alphabetically). That person will toss his or her object to another group member as you all say the memory verse together. Keep tossing the object around your group and repeating the verse. When I say, "Add one," the person with the next-longest first name will toss his or her object into the group. Then the group must juggle both items and repeat the verse. We'll keep doing this until you're juggling all four items in your group. If you drop an item, just pick it up and keep going. Ready? Go!

As groups juggle their items, allow about thirty seconds between times you say, "Add one." After the fourth item has entered into play, allow teenagers about a minute to master their juggling act.

Then have groups discuss the following questions:

- What was the hardest part of this game? the easiest? Why?
- Which was more important to you: juggling the objects or saying the Bible verse? Explain.
- If you had to grade how well you juggle "life" and "God," what grade would you give yourself? Why?

SAY:

- It's not easy to juggle everything and everyone in our lives, is it? And often we don't pay enough attention to our relationship with God. In fact, some of us even refuse to *begin* a relationship with God because we have no time for him. And some of us haven't even had time to realize our need for a relationship with God.
- Today we'll discuss how our activities distract us from God's ultimate purpose for us—growing close to God. Despite all the distractions in our lives, our commitment to God is what really matters.

◀ **The Point**

Seeds of Change
(25 to 30 minutes)

Bible Connection

Have groups of four remain together. Hand each student a pen and a copy of the "Seed and the Four Soils" handout.

SAY:

- We're going to explore a Bible story about growing in relationship with God. Before we begin, pray in your groups that God will use this story to teach you what he wants you to learn. You may pray aloud or silently.

When groups have finished praying, instruct group members to stand with their backs to each other, forming a square. Then have teenagers link elbows with the people on either side of them and push

against the rest of the group with their legs. While groups do this, read aloud Matthew 13:1-4, 19. When you've finished reading the passage, have groups sit down and discuss the questions and Bible passages under the "Hard Ground" section of the "Seed and the Four Soils" handout.

After five minutes, have each group form a circle. Instruct group members to turn so their right shoulders face the center of the circle, join their right hands and raise them above their heads, lift their right feet, and stand tiptoe on their left feet. While groups do this, read aloud Matthew 13:5-6, 20-21. Then have groups discuss the questions and Bible passages under the "Rocky Ground" section of the handout.

After five minutes, have groups stand in their own circles again. Instruct group members to put their hands around the neck of the person on the left. Make sure teenagers don't squeeze tightly! As teenagers do this motion, read aloud Matthew 13:7, 22. Then have groups discuss the questions and Bible passages under the "Thorny Ground" section of the handout.

After five minutes, have groups come up with a silent "cheer" such as doing the "wave." As groups do their cheers, read aloud Matthew 13:8, 23. Then have groups discuss the questions and Bible passages under the "Good Ground" section of the handout.

After five minutes, have groups discuss these questions:

- ■ How would you complete the sentence at the bottom of the handout? Why?
- ■ What does it mean to "produce fruit" in your life?
- ■ Based on what you've learned from this study, how does being a busy person affect your relationship with God?

SAY:

- ■ In the Bible story we just read, three of the four soils produced a plant but only one produced a crop. It's the same for people. Many of us may hear God's truth, but we don't allow it to go deep into our hearts and change us. When life troubles us, we turn to the familiar and tangible—things we recognize that we think can comfort us. We forget that our ultimate purpose in life is to be in a relationship with God.
- ■ The only way to produce lasting fruit in life is to follow God with everything you have in you. <u>Our commitment to God is what really matters</u>. The deeper your roots are in God, the greater your fruits will be in life.

The Point ▶

Thirsty Hearts
(15 to 20 minutes)

Have teenagers remain in their foursomes. Distribute a dried sponge to each student as well as scissors and a marker to each small group.

SAY:

■ The sponge I handed you represents your heart, so cut your sponge into a heart shape. Then, using the marker, write your name or initials in the middle of the heart shape.

Then have groups discuss these questions:

■ How hard was it to cut your heart shape? Why?
■ Why was the sponge hard? How did it get that way?
■ How is your sponge heart like your real heart? How is it different?
■ How might the distractions of life make your heart hard?

When groups have finished discussing the questions, give each group a water-filled paper cup labeled "Commitment to God."

SAY:

■ Sometimes, when we allow our lives to become so busy that we have no time to reflect or relax, our hearts become hard like your sponges. But God can soften our hearts, and when he does, we can fulfill our ultimate purpose in life—knowing him.
■ In a moment, you'll dip your sponge heart into the water. As you do, watch how your sponge changes. Think of how the water changing your sponge is like God changing your heart when you commit to him.

Invite teenagers to dip their sponge hearts into their cups of water. As they do, read aloud Matthew 13:23. Then have small groups discuss these questions:

■ How did your sponge heart change as you dipped it into the water?
■ How was the way the sponge changed like the way God can change your heart when you commit to him? How was it different?

Life Application

FYI

When Jesus used "sowing seed" as the foundation for his parable, he described a common sight in Palestine. In that time and culture, farmers sowed seed two ways. One strategy involved throwing the seed (often into the wind) to scatter it throughout a field. Another less common way was to trot a donkey with a bag of seed on its back down each row of a field. A small slit was cut in the bag, and the seed fell to the ground as the animal walked.

The "rocky ground" Jesus mentioned in this parable probably wasn't a layer of rocks but instead shelves of limestone just beneath a few inches of dirt. Upon such ground, seeds would sprout but not grow due to the soil's shallowness.

- Squeeze your sponge heart. How is water flowing from your sponge like what happens to your heart when you commit to God? How is it different?
- Do you want to know God better? Why or why not?
- How might you commit more deeply to God?

Invite groups to share their answers to the above questions. Then have each student move to a separate spot in the room.

SAY:

- I'm going to say a sentence for you to complete. After I say my part of the sentence, pray about how you'd complete it.
- An area in my life that tends to "choke" my relationship with God is...

After thirty seconds, have teenagers pray about their responses to this statement:

- To grow closer to God, I must help my roots grow strong. One way I can start doing this is...

After three minutes, have teenagers return to their foursomes to express any personal decisions they've made.

Before teenagers leave,

PRAY:

- Dear God, thank you for wanting us to grow closer to you. Please help us grow roots deep in you. Thank you for reminding us that our commitment to you is what really matters.

The Point ▶

FYI Some biblical scholars estimate that about one-third of Jesus' recorded teachings were parables. Parables are earthly stories that carry a heavenly meaning. The Greek root of the word *parable* means "to throw alongside" or "compare." Jesus unveiled the mysteries of God by likening them to earthly situations.

In the parable of the soils, Jesus compares seeds falling on different types of ground to people with varying spiritual commitments. Through this comparison, Jesus reveals several spiritual truths. First, not everyone who hears God's truth accepts it. Second, not all who accept it grow to maturity. Furthermore, spiritual growth is a long-term undertaking requiring patience and attention. And finally, we must develop proper foundations if we are to grow spiritually. The strength of our "roots" determines the quality and quantity of our "fruits."

The Seed and the Four Soils

The Hard Ground (Matthew 13:4)

1. What does Jesus say the hard ground represents (verse 19)? What eventually happened to the seed?

2. How was your physical pose similar to the hard ground and the type of person it represents? How was it different?

3. Read these Bible passages about people who fit into this category: King Pharaoh (Exodus 10:24-29) and King Agrippa (Acts 26:24-28). Based on these passages, what are three qualities of this type of person?

4. How might living a busy life contribute to someone being like hard ground?

5. Do you know anyone who fits this description? Have you ever fit it? When?

The Rocky Ground (Matthew 13:5-6)

1. What does Jesus say the rocky ground represents (verse 20-21)? What eventually happened to the seed?

2. How was your physical pose similar to the rocky ground and the type of person it represents? How was it different?

3. Read these Bible passages about people who fit into this category: King Saul (1 Samuel 28:15-19) and Judas Iscariot (Luke 22:1-6). Based on these passages, what are three qualities of this type of person?

4. How might living a busy life contribute to someone being like rocky ground?

5. Do you know anyone who fits this description? Have you ever fit it? When?

The Thorny Ground (Matthew 13:7)

1. What does Jesus say the thorny ground represents (verse 22)? What eventually happened to the seed?

2. How was your physical pose similar to the thorny ground and the type of person it represents? How was it different?

3. Read these Bible passages about people who fit into this category: King Solomon (1 Kings 10:23-25; 11:1-6) and the rich man (Luke 18:18-25). Based on these passages, what are three qualities of this type of person?

4. How might living a busy life contribute to someone being thorny ground?

5. Do you know anyone who fits this description? Have you ever fit it? When?

The Good Ground (Matthew 13:8)

1. What does Jesus say the good ground represents (verse 23)? What eventually happened to the seed?

2. How was your physical pose similar to the good ground and the type of person it represents? How was it different?

3. Read these Bible passages about people who fit into this category: Daniel (Daniel 6:1-5) and Joseph (Genesis 39:21-23). Based on these passages, what are three qualities of this type of person?

4. How might taking time out from a busy life contribute to someone being like good ground?

5. Do you know anyone who fits this description? Have you ever fit it? When?

The soil that best represents my present relationship with God (and why) is... _____

God's purpose for ME

Changed 4 Life

To keep your students thinking about God's purpose for them, try this idea at the end of this last study.

Give each person a pen and a piece of paper (use nice stationery if you have it). Ask students to write letters to themselves, outlining what they have learned in these Bible studies.

Encourage students to write down what they think God's purpose for them is and to outline specific ways they want to seek God's purpose and will for their lives.

When students have finished, ask them to put their letters in mailing envelopes and address them to themselves. Collect the letters and put them in a safe place.

A couple of months later, mail the letters to your students. Then the next time you get together, do a Bible study of how Bible characters discovered God's will for their lives. You might want to include these Scriptures: Judges 6:36-40; 1 Samuel 16:1-13; Matthew 4:18-22; and Acts 11:19-24. You also may want to have a time of discussion, letting teenagers talk in small groups about how they have been seeking and finding God's purpose for them.

To make this follow-up idea even more effective, make three copies of the students' letters and have them address four envelopes. Over the next year, mail them a copy of their letters every three months. Mail their original letters back to them after a year—then be sure to discuss them when you get together.

Look for the Whole Family of Faith 4 Life Bible Studies!

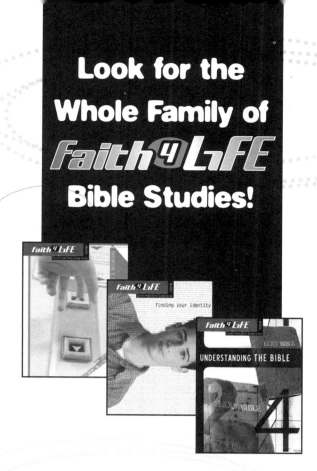

Senior High Books
- *Family Matters*
- *Is There Life After High School?*
- *Prayer*
- *Sharing Your Faith*

Junior High Books
- *Becoming a Christian*
- *Finding Your Identity*
- *God's Purpose for Me*
- *Understanding the Bible*

Preteen Books
- *Being Responsible*
- *Getting Along With Others*
- *God in My Life*
- *Going Through Tough Times*

Coming Soon!

for Senior High
- *Applying God's Word*
- *Christian Character*
- *Sexuality*
- *Your Christian ID*
- *Believing in Jesus*
- *Following Jesus*
- *Worshipping 24/7*
- *Your Relationships*

for Junior High
- *Choosing Wisely*
- *Friends*
- *My Family Life*
- *Sharing Jesus*
- *Fighting Temptation*
- *How to Pray*
- *My Life as a Christian*
- *Who Is God?*

for Preteens
- *Building Friendships*
- *How to Make Great Choices*
- *Succeeding in School*
- *What's a Christian?*
- *Handling Conflict*
- *Peer Pressure*
- *The Bible and Me*
- *Why God Made Me*

Visit your local Christian bookstore,
or contact Group Publishing, Inc., at 800-447-1070.
www.grouppublishing.com

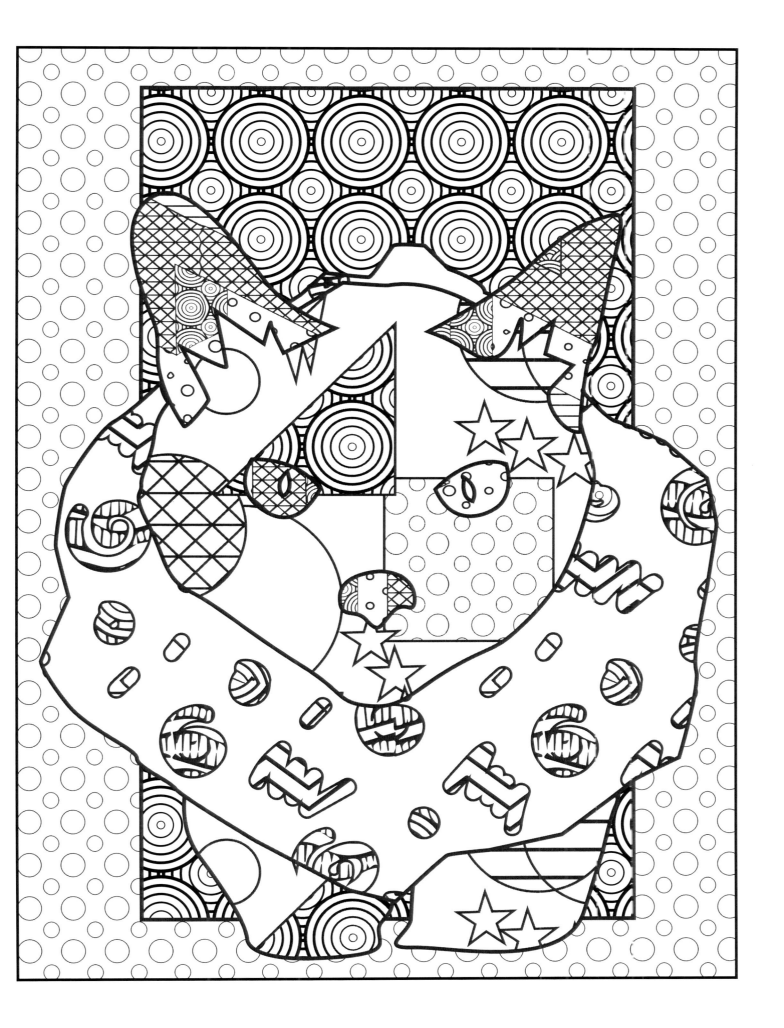

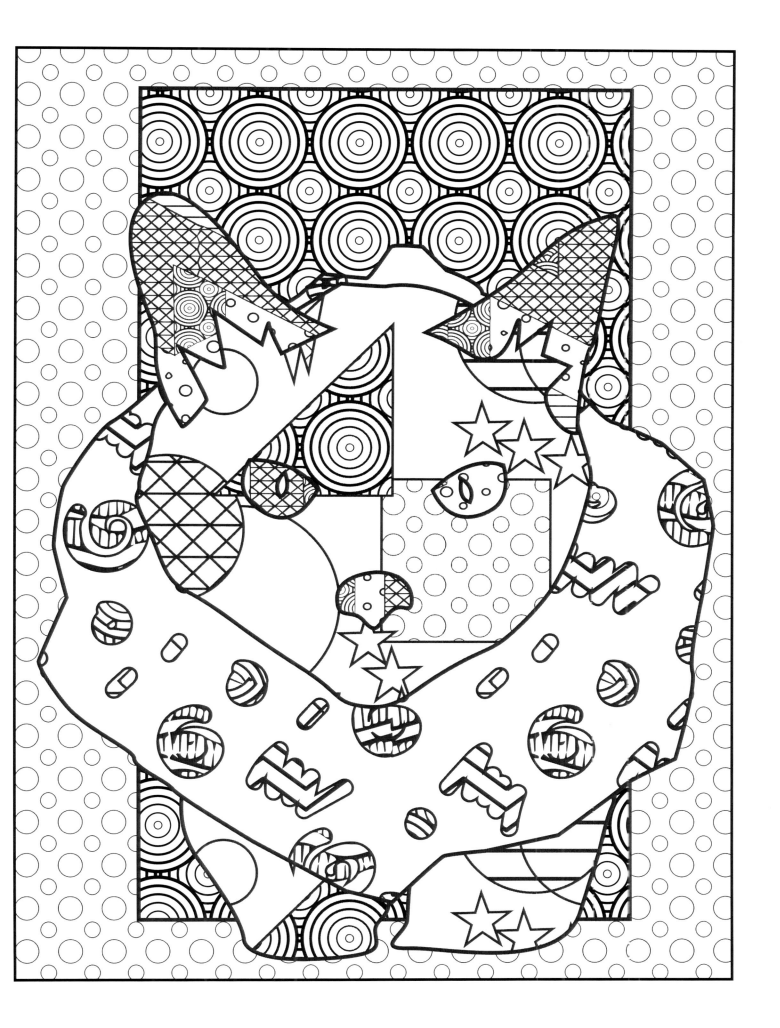

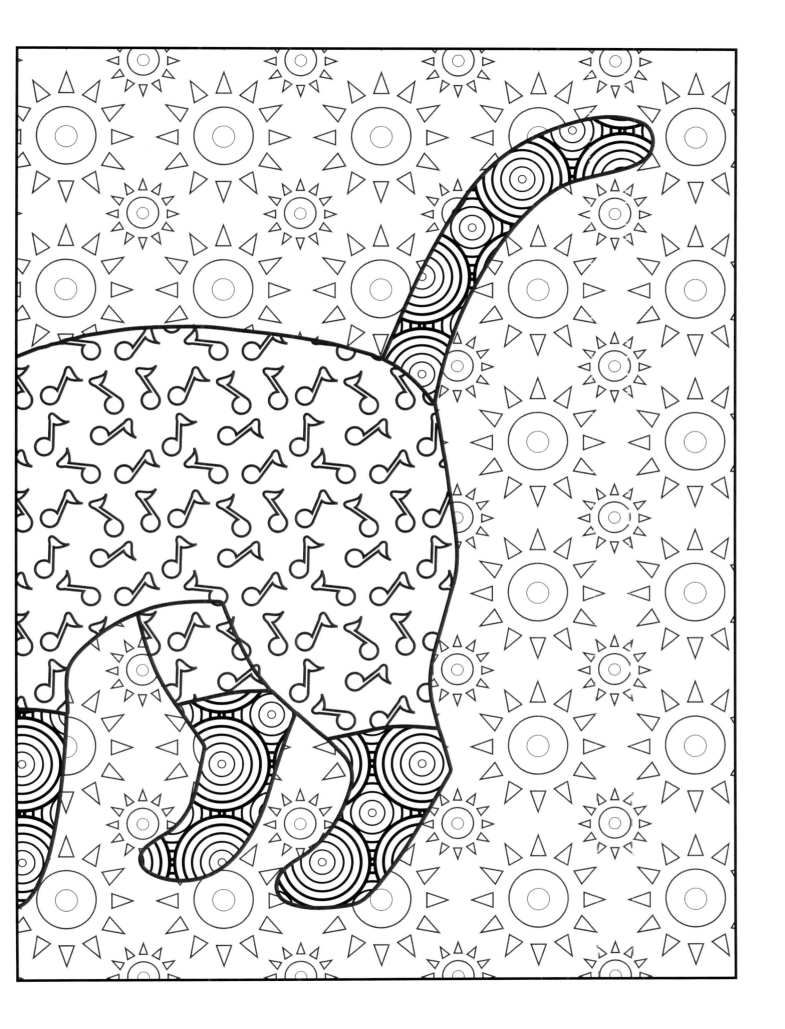

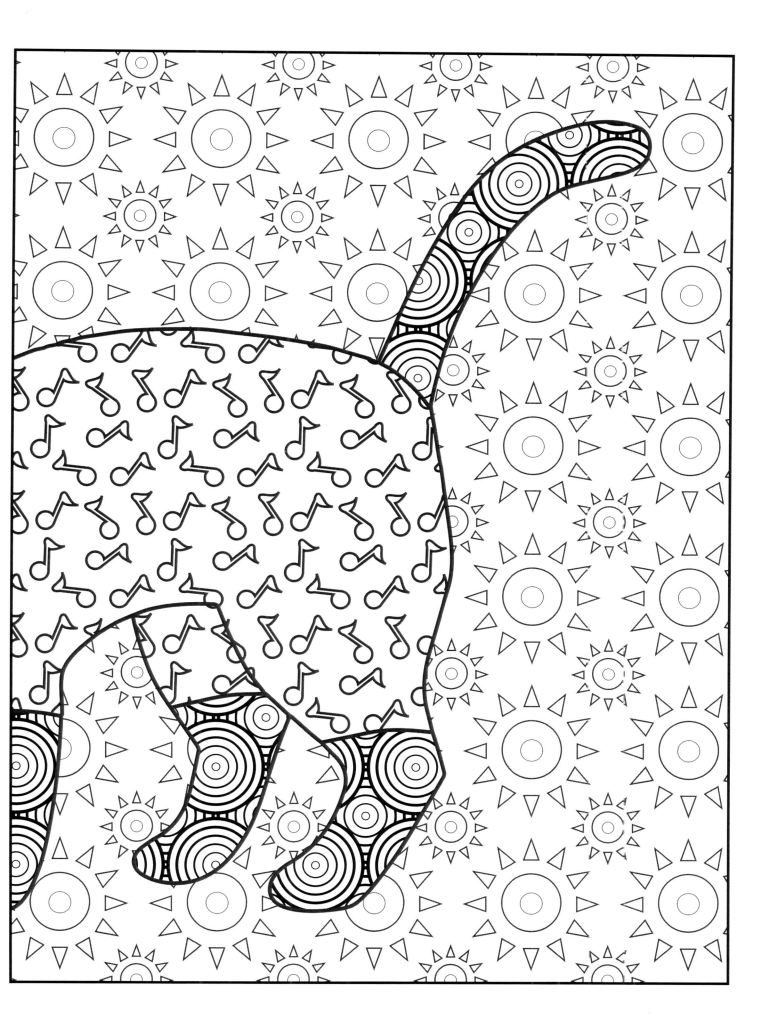

Made in United States
North Haven, CT
19 December 2021